Look What Came From

China

by

Miles Harvey

Franklin Watts

A Division of Grolier Publishing

New York London Hong Kong Sydney

Danbury, Connecticut

Series Concept: Shari Joffe
Design: Steve Marton

Library of Congress Cataloging-in-Publication Data

Harvey, Miles.
   Look What Came From China / by Miles Harvey.
     p. cm. — (Look what came from)
   Includes bibliographical references and index.
   Summary: Describes many things, both familiar and
unfamiliar, that originally came from China, including
inventions, food, tools, animals, toys, games, musical
instruments, fashion, medicine, and sports.
   ISBN 0-531-11495-3
   1. China — Civilization — Juvenile literature.
   2. Civilization — Chinese influences — Juvenile literature.
   [1. China — Civilization.] I. Title. II. Series.
   DS721.H323   1988
   951 — dc21
                                                    97-35689
                                                       CIP
                                                        AC

© 1998 Franklin Watts, a Division of Grolier Publishing.
All rights reserved. Published simultaneously in Canada.
Printed in Mexico
11 12 13 14 15 R 10 09 08 07 06 05

Photo credits © : Animals, Animals: 3 top, 15 middle (Max Gibbs); Art Resource:
19 left (Erich Lessing); Bonhams, London/Bridgeman Art Library Intl. Ltd.,
London/New York: border on pages 4, 6-32 (Chinese dragon robe, 19th century,
embroidered terracotta silk); Ann Chwatsky: 3 bottom, 20 right, 21 right, 24, 27;
Charise Mericle: 5; ChinaStock: back cover stamp, 4 middle, 4 right, 8 left,
9 right, 11, 22 middle (Dennis Cox), 7 middle, 17 right (Christopher Liu),
16 (Liu Qijun), 6 top, 6 bottom; Corbis-Bettmann: 7 left, 13 left, 20 left;
H. Armstrong Roberts: 25 left (C. Ursillo), 25 right; The Image Works: 17 left
(Jim Pickerell); Jay Mallin Photos: 32 left (Jay Mallin); Jeffrey Aaronson/
Network Aspen: 23 left; PhotoEdit: front cover bottom left, 18 left (D. Young-
Woolf), 8 right (Jeff Greenberg), 22 right (Gary A. Conner), 23 right (Amy C.
Etra); Rengin Altay: 32 right; Science Museum/Science & Society Picture Library:
13 right; SuperStock: 4 left (Y. F. Chan), 12 left, 15 right (Christie's Images),
front cover background, front cover top right, 6 left, 18 right, 21 left; Tony Stone
Worldwide: 7 right (David Sutherland), 10 right (Steven Rothfeld), 12 right
(Don Smetzer), 14 left (Keren Su), 19 right (D. E. Cox), 22 left (Paul Chesley),
26 (Lawrence Migdale), front cover bottom right, 9 left, 10 left, 15 left

Contents

China, a Great Place

China is an amazing place. It has more people than any other country in the world. Nearly 1.2 billion people live there! China also covers more land than any country except Russia and Canada. In addition, China has one of the world's oldest civilizations.

The flag of China

China is on the continent of Asia. It is thousands of miles from the United States. To get there, you would have to go all the way across the Pacific Ocean. But if you want to learn about China, you don't really have to take a trip. That's because many things in your everyday life were invented in China—including the paper that these words are printed on.

So, come on! Let's find out about all the cool things that come from China!

Chinese paper money and coins

Inventions

Some very important inventions have come from China. For example, about 2,500 years ago, people in China came up with a special tool to help them with math. This invention became known as the **abacus.** It was the earliest kind of computer!

Ancient Chinese people making paper pulp

Nearly 1,900 years ago, a man who worked for the emperor of China invented **paper.** He made it out of pulp made from fish nets, rags, and plants. Today, paper is usually made out of tree pulp.

Abacus

Ancient Chinese people drying pulp on frames

The Chinese also figured out a special way to apply ink to paper. This invention was called **printing.** These days, we use printing to make books, newspapers, magazines, posters, and money.

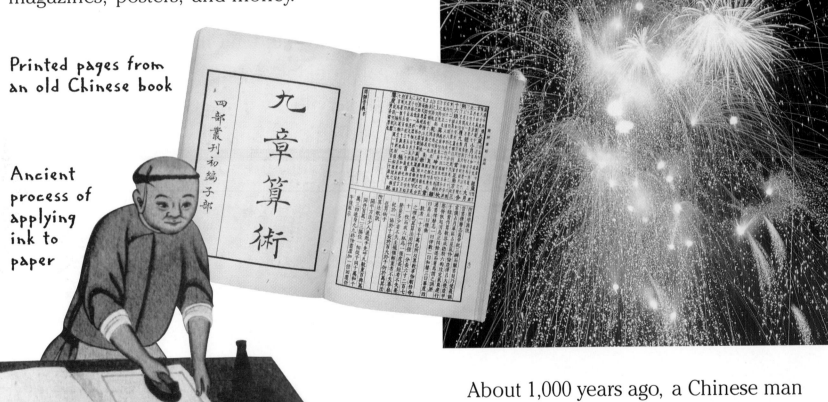

Printed pages from an old Chinese book

Ancient process of applying ink to paper

About 1,000 years ago, a Chinese man mixed some different chemicals together. They began to spark and explode. He had invented **fireworks!**

Some of the most familiar foods on your table were first eaten in China. Did you know that people in China have been growing and eating **rice** for more than 7,000 years? Rice is an important part of Chinese cooking and is served with many different kinds of meals.

Food

Tea, a popular drink throughout the world, was also invented in China. People in China began drinking tea almost 5,000 years ago. Some people say that a Chinese emperor discovered the drink when leaves from a tea plant blew into his pot of boiling water!

Rice

Chinese tea seller

Soybean plants

The Chinese love **soybeans.** They use them to create soy sauce, which they sprinkle on their food. They also use soybeans to make a very healthy food called tofu. Farmers in China have been growing soybeans for about 5,000 years. Now many American farmers also grow these amazing beans.

Tofu, soy sauce, and soybeans

more

The Chinese were also the first people to discover the delicious flavor of the **peach**. A long time ago, some people in China thought that by eating a lot of peaches you would live forever!

They were wrong about that. But they were right about peaches being very good for you.

Peach

Ice cream

About 4,000 years ago, the Chinese came up with one of the most yummy foods ever invented—**ice cream!** They used rice, milk, spices, and snow to create the treat. We use different ingredients today, but the results are still delicious!

10

food

A lot of people think that people in Italy invented **pasta.** Actually, people in China came up with the idea for pasta at least 3,000 years ago.

Pasta

Tools

The Chinese invented lots of tools you may have used or seen. For example, a **saddle** makes riding a horse comfortable and easy. This tool was invented in China nearly 2,000 years ago.

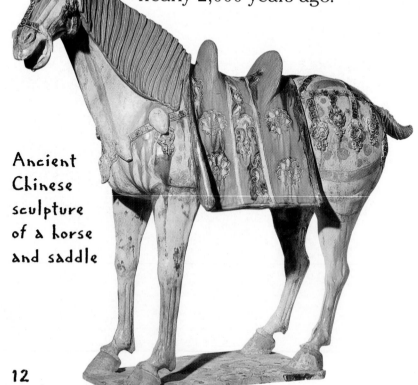

Ancient Chinese sculpture of a horse and saddle

Chopsticks

People in China do not usually use knives, forks, or spoons to eat their food. They use two special pieces of wood called **chopsticks.** You can try to use chopsticks when you go to a Chinese restaurant.

Wheelbarrow

The **compass** is a tool that helps people find out which direction they are going. Many people believe that the Chinese invented the compass about 1,000 years ago. Christopher Columbus used a compass on his trip to America in 1492.

About 1,700 years ago, a man in the Chinese army invented a special kind of cart that had only one wheel. This invention became known as the **wheelbarrow.** Today, people use wheelbarrows to move dirt, stones, and plants in their gardens.

Compass

Animals

You may not realize it, but China is the home of several animals you know. The **giant panda** is one very famous animal that comes from China. But only a few of these beautiful animals still remain. Many people are trying to make sure the giant pandas survive.

The **Pekingese** is a kind of dog that came from China more than 2,000 years ago. Chinese emperors used to keep these dogs as pets. Another dog that comes from China is the **shar-pei.** The shar-pei has very loose, wrinkly skin.

Pekingese

Giant panda

14

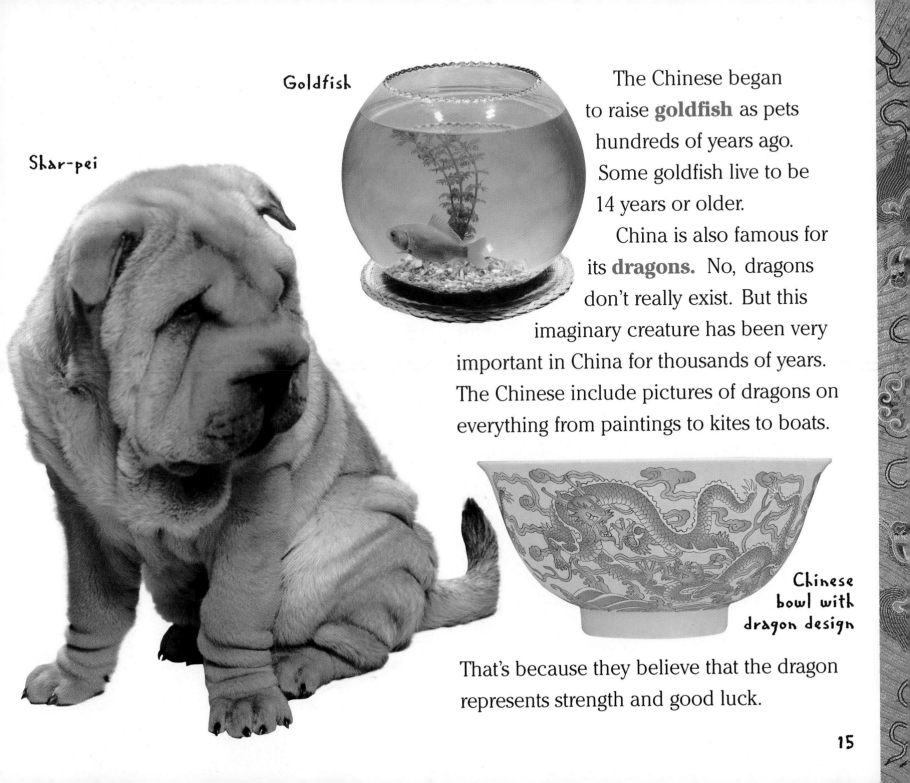

Goldfish

Shar-pei

The Chinese began to raise **goldfish** as pets hundreds of years ago. Some goldfish live to be 14 years or older.

China is also famous for its **dragons.** No, dragons don't really exist. But this imaginary creature has been very important in China for thousands of years. The Chinese include pictures of dragons on everything from paintings to kites to boats.

Chinese bowl with dragon design

That's because they believe that the dragon represents strength and good luck.

15

Toys and Games

Have you ever flown a **kite?** The Chinese invented kites more than 3,000 years ago. People in China still love to fly them. They make brightly colored kites in the shapes of butterflies, birds, tadpoles, and dragons.

Chinese kite makers

Dominoes

For more than 2,000 years, kids in China have been playing a fun game with their feet. The object of this game is to keep a little ball in the air as long as possible. In the United States, we call this game **hacky sack**.

Ancient Chinese drawing of children playing the game we call hacky sack

But kites aren't the only fun toys that come from China. Have you ever played **dominoes?** They were invented in China about 1,000 years ago. Today, dominoes are just a game. But back then, some people used them to try to tell the future!

Arts and Crafts

Chinese fan

The Chinese also made the world's first **carpets** about 2,500 years ago. Chinese artists still create beautiful rugs.

Chinese rug

Take a look around your house—it may be decorated with things that come from China! That's because the Chinese invented some beautiful crafts that are now found around the world.

People in China began making **fans** about 5,000 years ago. Many Chinese fans are covered with beautiful paintings. Today, some people hang these fans on their walls as decoration.

People in China have long been making beautiful pottery. One of the most famous kinds of Chinese pottery is called **porcelain.** For hundreds of years, porcelain was a secret. No one outside of China could figure out how to make it!

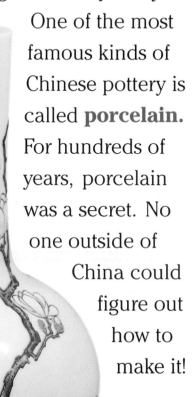

Porcelain

Chinese calligraphy

People in China use a much different kind of writing than we do. Chinese writing is very beautiful, but it is hard to do well. That's why the Chinese consider writing a kind of art. The name of this art is **calligraphy.**

19

Musical Instruments

Ancient Chinese bell

The Chinese also make some instruments that are similar to some instruments you might know. One is an instrument similar to the fiddle. But instead of having four strings, this only has two. In China, such a fiddle is called an *erhu.*

Have you ever rung a **bell?** This instrument was invented in China more than 3,000 years ago. The first bells were made out of a kind of metal called bronze.

Children playing the erhu

Boy playing a ch'in

One of the oldest
Chinese instruments
is played with the
mouth. It is similar
to the harmonica,
and is called
a **sheng.**

A lute is an instrument similar to the
guitar. One kind of Chinese instrument is
called the moon lute. It is round like the
moon. In China, it is called a **ch'in.**

Boy
playing a
sheng

Fashion

You may not know it, but you've probably worn things that were invented in China. Do your parents have any clothes or scarves made out of **silk?** Silk is a very smooth kind of fabric. People in China have been making silk for more than 3,000 years. The silk threads come from the cocoon of a caterpillar called a silkworm.

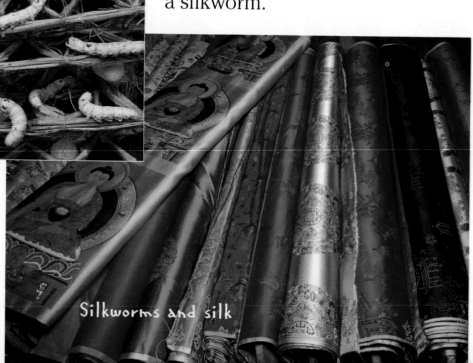

Silkworms and silk

Modern sunglasses

Do you like wearing **sunglasses?** The Chinese invented them more than 500 years ago.

Medicine

Chinese medicine is thousands of years old. But it is still practiced in many parts of the world—including North America.

Chinese doctors are a lot like American doctors. But some kinds of Chinese medicine are different from ours. One of them is called **acupuncture.** In acupuncture, many tiny needles are inserted into a person's body to relieve pain or cure an illness. Believe it or not, this treatment doesn't hurt!

Ginseng on sale at a Chinese market

Today, many Americans use acupuncture.

The Chinese also believe that certain plants can help you stay healthy. These plants are known as herbs. One famous herb is called **ginseng.** Many people drink a special tea made from this herb, but you can also find ginseng in some kinds of soft drinks. Ginseng is supposed to give you lots of energy.

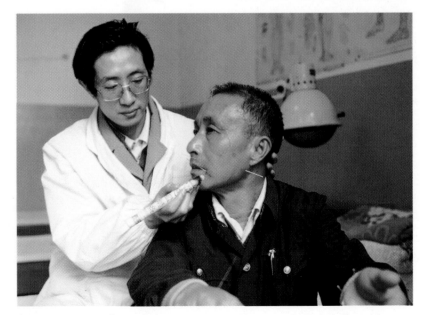

Doctor performing acupuncture on a patient

23

Sports and Exercise

Children practicing kung fu

Many of China's physical arts have made their way to the United States. One very famous Chinese sport is a special type of boxing known as *kung fu.* This sport is very difficult. To become good at it, you have to practice for many years.

Tai chi

A popular kind of exercise in China is known as **tai chi.** It is very good for you. It is also very interesting to watch. People who do tai chi sometimes look as if they are dancing in slow motion.

For more than 2,000 years, people in China have been doing a sport called **acrobatics.** People who are acrobats perform amazing tricks. Some of them juggle things in the air. Others pile objects up very high, then balance themselves on top of these objects. No wonder people love to go see acrobats at the circus!

Chinese acrobats

25

A Recipe from China

Fried rice is a popular meal in China. You can use a lot of different ingredients in this delicious dish. That's why Chinese people sometimes use whatever leftovers they have around the kitchen. Do you want to try cooking fried rice? Great!

Simple Fried Rice

Chinese people use a special bowl-shaped pan called a *wok* to make fried rice. But if you don't have a wok, you can use any large, deep pan. To start, you'll need the following ingredients:

4 cups of cold cooked rice

4 eggs

1/4 cup of chopped-up scallions
(a kind of onion)

2 tablespoons of water

3 to 4 tablespoons of vegetable oil

1/2 teaspoon of salt

1/2 teaspoon of sugar

a dash of pepper

2 tablespoons of soy sauce

You can do the following part of the recipe by yourself, with an adult watching.

1. Wash your hands—then use them to break up the clumps of the cold cooked rice until it is no longer lumpy.

2. Being very careful with a knife, chop up the scallions into tiny pieces.

3. Break the eggs into a bowl and add the water.

4. Add the 1/4 cup of chopped-up scallions.

5. Lightly beat the eggs, scallions, and water until they are well mixed.

You'll need an adult to do the next part of the recipe, but you can help out by reading the instructions out loud.

1. Heat the oil in the wok or large, deep pan. The oil should be very hot. Wait until it starts to smoke before adding the ingredients.

2. Add the rice to the pan. While stirring it with a spatula, cook it until all of it is hot.

3. Add the salt and pepper.

4. Pour the eggs into the pan and stir them into the rice. Keep stirring.

5. When the eggs are cooked, the fried rice is done. Now all you have to do is put a few more chopped scallions on the top, then sprinkle on some soy sauce. And you're ready to eat!

Once you learn how to make basic fried rice, you can add different ingredients. The Chinese like to put in meats like beef, pork, chicken, or duck. They also add vegetables—everything from peas to mushrooms to bean sprouts to bamboo shoots. You can add whatever you like—that's the fun of fried rice!

How do you say....?

China is such a big place that many different languages are spoken there. The official language is called Mandarin. As you can see, words in Mandarin look much different from words in English.

English	Mandarin	How to pronounce it
dog	狗	go
fan	扇子	shanzi
fish	鱼	yu
goodbye	再见	dzay jenn
hello	你好	nee how
ice cream	冰淇淋	beeng-jee-leen
kite	风筝	feng-zheng
paper	纸	jee
peach	桃子	taozi
tea	茶	cha

To find out more

Here are some other resources to help you learn more about China:

Books

Cotterell, Arthur. **Ancient China.** Eyewitness Books, Knopf, 1994.

Kalman, Bobbie. **China: The Culture.** Crabtree Publishing Company, 1989.

Keeler, Stephen. **Passport to China.** Franklin Watts, 1994.

The Nature Company. **Ancient China.** Time-Life Books, 1996.

Waterlow, Julia. **China.** Franklin Watts, 1989.

Organizations and Online Sites

China—CityNet
http://www.city.net/countries/china/
Find out today's weather in China—and take a look at a great list of web links about the country.

China Maps
http://www.lib.utexas.edu/Libs/PCL/Map_collection/china.html
Check out this cool collection of online maps of China, provided by the University of Texas at Austin.

China National Tourist Office, New York
350 Fifth Avenue, Suite 6413
Empire State Building
New York, NY 10118
http://www.welleslian.com/dragontour/frame.html

China National Tourist Office, Los Angeles
333 West Broadway, Suite 201
Glendale, CA 91204

For Kids Only: Facts About China
http://nis.accel.worc.k12.ma.us/WWW/Projects/China/kidschina.html
Learn basic information about China, including facts about the famous Great Wall.

The Land of Beauty
http://www.cnd.org:8029/Scenery/
Visit a great collection of beautiful online photographs of China.

Glossary

abacus an ancient tool used for doing math problems

acrobat a performer who does juggling and balancing tricks

acupuncture a Chinese medical treatment in which the skin is punctured with tiny needles at specific points to cure diseases or relieve pain

ancestor a relative who lived in the past

calligraphy the art of beautiful handwriting

chopsticks sticks the Chinese use instead of knives, forks, and spoons

civilization the way of life of a people

cocoon a home spun by certain insects for protection while they change from a larva into an adult insect

continent one of the major land areas of the earth

emperor ruler of an empire

ginseng a type of plant that many Chinese think is good for your health

lacquer a special kind of paint that makes things shiny

lute a type of musical instrument similar to the guitar or zither

porcelain a type of pottery invented by the Chinese

pulp a material prepared from wood or rags that is used in making paper

tofu a healthy kind of food made out of soy beans

wok a bowl-shaped cooking pan used in China

Index

Look what doesn't come from China!

When you go to a Chinese restaurant, you're likely to get a **fortune cookie**. But fortune cookies weren't invented in China. They come from the United States! No one knows who came up with the idea. But some people think a man in Los Angeles named David Jung made the first fortune cookies about eighty years ago. He gave the treats to poor and homeless people to cheer them up.

Meet the Author

Miles Harvey is the author of several books for young people. He lives in Chicago. This book is dedicated to Carter and Glenna Gee-Taylor, whose grandparents are two of the great things that come from China.